THE MATARESE CIRCLE

MATARSE CÍRCULO

my cameo as a poet in a cold war spy novel

To Dana

Matarse Círculo
my cameo as a poet in a cold war spy novel

Thanks to Pablo, Xun, Kid Spandex, Teacher Li, Jefe Collins, Hoss, Mom.

Original limited edition produced in Chiapas, México, August 2022, with hand-stitched cartón binding by Andrew Long.

This expanded trade edition published in 2024.

ISBN: 978-1-63752-414-5

© Scott Ezell, 2024

not somewhat relieved that the Soviet Union has lost its foremost nuclear physicist."

"I am not, sir. His brilliance transcended our borders and differences. He was a man for all peoples."

"Yet he chose to be a part of *one* people, did he not? I tell you frankly, my concerns do not transcend our differences. Rather, they force me to look to my flanks."

"Then, if you'll forgive me, Mr. Premier, you're looking for phantoms."

"Perhaps we've found them, Mr. President. We have evidence that is extremely disturbing to me. So much so that I have—"

"Forgive me once again," interrupted the President of the United States. "Your evidence has prompted my calling you, in spite of my natural reluctance to do so. The KGB has made a great error. Four errors, to be precise."

"Four?"

"Yes, Mr. Premier. Specifically the names Scofield, Randolph, Saltzman and Bergstrom. None was involved, Mr. Premier."

"You astonish me, Mr. President."

"No more than you astonished me the other week. There are fewer secrets these days, remember?"

"Words are inexpensive; the evidence is strong."

"Then it's been so calculated. Let me clarify. Two of the three men from Central Intelligence are no longer in sanction. Randolph and Bergstrom are currently at their desks in Washington. Mr. Saltzman was hospitalized in Tashkent; the diagnosis is cancer." The President paused.

"That leaves one name, doesn't it?" said the Premier. "Your man from the infamous Consular Operations. So bland in diplomatic circles, but infamous to us."

"This is the most painful aspect of my clarification. It's inconceivable that Mr. Scofield could have been involved. There was less chance of his involvement than any of the others, frankly. I tell you this because it no longer matters."

"Words cost little—"

"I must be explicit. For the past several years a covert, in-depth dossier has been maintained on Dr. Yurievich, information added

33

PART I

33
Look to your flank
look to the phantoms in your heart
choose your poison and your pain
choose the first-class red-eye
to Tashkent or Ulaan Baatar
we could go sturgeon fishing in Lake Baikal
with 20,000 years of human ruins
strewn along the shore
trolling the depths with a
line and a barb
floating on the surface
while a mile of shadows
abides beneath—

forgive me forgive me
what else can I say
to my hands
to the nuclear distance
between them and touch and you
my flank is a traitor
and sags like an animal skin
wet-salted
nailed to a barn door
then forgotten 20 years
despite my natural reticence
I have no secrets
to die for or conceal—

forgive me I said again
to the president and his secret agents
and to every cell
of my body
central intelligence is no longer
at its desk
the diagnosis was cancer
words are inexpressive
and so bland in diplomatic circles
I used a hacksaw for the jawbone
and threw the teeth into the well

my hands are empty
and can't transcend our distances
but thank you for your frankness
we must look to other flanks.

THE MATARESE CIRCLE

The old woman stared straight ahead. "You have what you came for, signori. Take it. Take her. Leave!"

Bray turned to the girl. "We owe her that," he said. He grabbed the shotgun out of her hands. She tried to fight back but Taleniekov pinned her arms and removed the Browning and the Graz-Burya automatics from her pockets. "You saw what happened down there," continued Scofield. "Do as she says."

The dog raced to the open door and barked viciously. Far in the distance, voices were carried on the morning breezes; men were shouting to others behind them.

"Go!" said Sophia Pastorine.

"Come on." Bray propelled Antonia in front of him. "We'll be back after they've left. We haven't finished."

"A moment, signori!" shouted the blind woman. "I think we have finished. The names you possess may be helpful to you, but they are only the inheritors. Look for the one whose voice is crueler than the wind. I heard it! Find him. The shepherd boy. It is he!"

257

257
Take the money and leave
the old woman said
as the dogs brayed
and I fingered the automatic in my pocket
the soldiers laughed
as they poured salt in the well
tracks cross a ridge of snow
piss stains in the bootprints
the forest became a golf course
but still something waits for spring
beneath a glaze of ice
I strapped the blade to my thigh
just to feel cold metal against my skin
you have what you came for the old woman said
though I hadn't eaten for three days—

what is crueler than the wind
that comes and goes
and shouts like a man
who never touches earth
only laughs with blood joy blood lust
the dogs run across the hill
far from fealty or love
blackbird thoughts
scatter across the sky
in a crooked line
go
come
go
you saw what happened
the old woman said
the tracks lead to the border
you'll reach it when you have
nowhere else to go.

"What are you thinking?" asked Taleniekov.

"She said we'd finished. We *haven't*. But she's going to make sure of it! They'll see our footprints on the floor; we walked over wet ground; she can't deny we were there. With her hearing, she knows which way we went. She'll send them in another direction."

"That's fine," said the Russian.

"Godamn it, they'll *kill* her!"

Taleniekov snapped his head back toward the farmhouse below. "You're right," he said. "If they believe her—and they will—they can't let her live. She's the source; she'll tell them that, too, if only to convince them. Her life for the shepherd boy. So we can find the shepherd boy!"

"But we don't *know* enough! Come on, let's go!" Scofield got to his feet, yanking the automatic from his belt. The dog snarled; the girl rose and Taleniekov pushed her down to the ground again.

They were not in time. Three gunshots followed one upon the other.

Antonia screamed; Bray lunged, holding her, cradling her. "*Please*, please!" he whispered. He saw the Russian pull a knife from somewhere inside his coat. "*No!* It's all right!"

Taleniekov palmed the knife and knelt down, his eyes on the farmhouse below. "They're running outside. You were right; they're heading for the south slope."

"Kill them!" The girl's words were muffled by Scofield's hand.

"To what purpose now?" said the KGB man. "She did what she wished to do, what she felt she had to do."

The dog would not follow them; commands from Antonia had no effect. It raced down into the farmhouse and would not come out; its whimpering carried up to the ridge.

"Goodbye, Uccello," said the girl sobbing. "I will come back for you. Before *God*, I will come back!"

They walked out of the mountains, circling northwest beyond the hills of Porto Vecchio, then south to Sainte Lucie, following the stream until they reached the massive pine under which Bray

260
The jolly Russian pulled a knife out
gunshots rang out one by one
a down-syndrome Saint Bernard
came bounding through the snow
strands of drool swinging from its snout
the Russian opened a flask and said
have a shot of brandy for that
broken leg
it won't cure you but it won't kill you—

there's an masochistic pleasure to
cigarettes in the anthropocene
like gambling an inheritance you never received
on a coin flipped from a satellite
to fall through the stratosphere to earth
damned if we'll ever find it
but if we do I guess we'll know who won
which side did you call again?

I don't know why I'm typing
on these old pages
with this old machine
but I never knew enough of anything
to say what's right or wrong
so I just give what I can
as I walk through the rose garden
a few coins for the beggars
drops of water for the wilting leaves—

the Saint Bernard simpered
its pink erection melting through the snow
the Russian stroked his cigarette
smoke leapt in the wind
he put the knife in his pocket and
took out a coin
call it he said
but I didn't know which side was up or down
or if gravity would ever be on my side again
I wished I was on the Titanic

on the top deck
driving golf balls out to sea
I would have aimed for the iceberg
I would have aimed for a hole in one
I'd call fore! across the water
even if
there was no one there to hear, there there.

THE MATARESE CIRCLE

Ortiz Ortega, Madrid; he's crossed out. Josua—which is presumed to be Joshua—Appleton, State of Massachusetts, America. The Spaniard was killed by the *padrone* at Villa Matarese, so he was never part of the council. The remaining four have long since died, but two of their descendants are very prominent, very available. David Waverly and Joshua Appleton the fourth. Britain's Foreign Secretary and the senator from Massachusetts. I say we go for immediate confrontation."

"I don't," said Bray, looking down at the paper and the childlike writing of the letters. "Because we do know who they are, and we don't know anything about the others. Who are their descendants? Where are they? If there're more surprises, let's try to find them first. The Matarese isn't restricted to two men, and these two in particular may have nothing to do with it."

"Why do you say that?"

"Everything I know about both of them would seem to deny anything like the Matarese. Waverly had what they call in England a 'good war'; a young commando, highly decorated. Then a hell of a record in the Foreign Office. He's always been a tactical compromiser, not an inciter; it doesn't fit. . . . Appleton's a Boston Brahmin who bolted the class lines and became a liberal reformer for three terms in the Senate. Protector of the working man as well as the intellectual community. He's a shining knight on a solid, political horse that most of America thinks will take him to the White House next year."

"What better residence for a *consigliere* of the Matarese?"

"It's too jarring, too pat. I think he's genuine."

"The art of conviction—in both instances, perhaps. But you're right: they won't vanish. So we start in Leningrad and Rome, trace what we can."

" 'You and *yours* will do what I can no longer do. . . .' Those were the words Matarese used seventy years ago. I wonder if it's that simple."

"Meaning the 'yours' could be selected, not born?" asked Taleniekov. "Not direct descendants?"

"Yes."

273

The transmission was intercepted
the entire operation jeopardized
insurgents blew a train up in Madrid
and put cyanide in the commander's wineskin
but the real confrontation is oblique
the puppet masters never appear
only dancing girls and drummer boys pass by
as animal sounds of anguish or ecstasy
emerge from behind the curtain
it's a shell game of broken lives
but I think if you touched me one more time
I'd relinquish everything else in the world—

the last recon plane crashed
under suspicious circumstances
it didn't matter
I already held
the surveillance file in my pocket
and the tracking device
was sewn into my eyes

the Trojan horse waits
outside the palace gate
terrified soldiers crouch in the dark
praying to their mothers
praying to be born heroes not corpses
from the womb of the mechanized animal
but the mercenary with the guitar
plays only love songs

I wrote a poem to you in morse code
with needle marks in my arm
do what you can no longer do
be what there's no hope left to be
you can't return
to the belly of the beast
except with an adze and a blade
to kill it from within
and you'll expire with it either way
somewhere on the last piece of unmapped earth
the wreckage of the last recon plane
is rusting back to soil.

THE MATARESE CIRCLE

sitting next to him, dressed in khaki trousers and a torn field jacket was the same woman who had been so sullen and unresponsive. Or who had shouted orders in the hills and handled the Lupo so efficiently. They had several minutes left before going into the lifeboat, so he asked her about the Lupo.

"I went through a phase, we all do, I think. A time when drastic social change seems possible only through violence. Those maniacs from the Brigate Rosse knew how to play us."

"The Brigades? You were with the *Red Brigades?* Good *Lord!*"

She nodded. "I spent several weeks at a Brigatisti camp in Medicina, learning how to fire weapons, and scale walls and hide contraband—none of which I did particularly well, incidentally— until one morning when a young student, a boy, really, was killed in what the leaders called a 'training accident.' A *training accident*, such a *military* sound, but they were not soldiers. Only brutes and bullies, let loose with knives and guns. He died in my arms, the blood flowing from his wound . . . his eyes so frightened and bewildered. I hardly knew him but when he died, I couldn't stand it. Guns and knives and clubs were not the way; that night I left and returned to Bologna.

"So what you saw in Porto Vecchio was an act. It was dark, and you did not see the fear in my eyes."

He had been right. She was not for the barricades; there would be no merry month of May for her.

"You know," he said slowly, "we're going to be together for a while."

There was no fear in her eyes now. "We have not settled that question, have we?"

"What question?"

"Where I'm going. You and the Russian said I was to trust you, do as you were doing, leave Corsica and say nothing. Well, signore, we've left Corsica and I've trusted you. I didn't run away."

"Why didn't you?"

Antonia paused briefly. "Fear, and you know it. You're not normal men. You speak courteously, but you move too quickly for

277

Gulls circle above the waste dump
chips of alabaster against the oystershell sky
no lifeboats
as the coast erodes
unloosing scrap metal and plastic dolls
into the currents of the sea
you didn't see the fear in my eyes
no one saw it in anyone's
we were too enthralled with scintillations
in the house of mirrors
reflecting endless impossible futures—

in his khaki trousers and torn field jacket
he frowned at the typewriter and thought
I should have learned to fire weapons
and scale walls instead
but the resistance was eliminated long ago
and I was never one for the barricades...

the old cottage on the cliffs above the sea
was once a dream
now it's another piece of wreckage
joining the flow of the buried past
no one wanted to see
blue efflux of salt and time
human flotsam emerging from oblivion
and merging back again
but I think
we should try to get along
you never know
we might still be here
for a while.

you said you didn't run away before because you were afraid to, not because you trusted us. That's being honest. You brought us up to Bastia. Be honest with me now. Knowing what you know—seeing what you saw in Porto Vecchio—how good is your word?"

At midships, the lifeboat was being hoisted over the railing by four crewmen; Antonia watched it as she spoke. "You're being unfair. You know what I saw, and you know what you told me. When I think about it, I want to cry out and. . . ." She did not finish; instead she turned back to him, her voice weary. "How good is my word? I don't know. So what's left for me? Will it be you and not the Russian who fires the bullet?"

"I may offer you a job."

"I don't want work from you."

"We'll see," said Bray.

"*Venite subito, signori. La lancia va partire.*"

The lifeboat was in the water. Scofield reached for the duffle bag at his side and got to his feet. He held out his hand for Antonia. "Come on. I've had easier people to deal with."

The statement was true. He could kill this woman if he had to. Still, he would try not to have to.

Where was the new life for Beowulf Agate now?

God, he hated this one.

Bray hired a taxi in Fiumicino, the driver at first reluctant to accept a fare to Rome, changing his mind instantly at the sight of the money in Scofield's hand. They stopped for a quick meal and still reached the inner city before eight o'clock. The streets were crowded, the shops doing a brisk evening's business.

"Pull up in that parking space," said Bray to the driver. They were in front of a clothing store. "Wait here," he added, including Antonia in the command. "I'll guess your size." He opened the door.

"What are you doing?" asked the girl.

"A transition," replied Scofield in English. "You can't walk into a decent shop dressed like that."

Five minutes later he returned carrying a box containing denim

279

Well
Beowulf never had to
put up with this shit
hummingbirds sucking nectar
from plastic flowers
the lifeboat lonely as a leper
bobbing on the open sea
the revolver always in someone else's hand—

maybe we'll meet in Porto Vecchio
I'll be the one in the scarlet cravat
but for now spot me a hunski for the baccarat table
the crewmen had knives in their boots
any one could have dispatched the Russian
come aboard come aboard
you have no choice
you're not an albatross nor were meant to be
get your sugar from the plastic feeder
like the rest of us
mold yourself a new self from the
ripples of the sea
they're a valuable resource
soon they'll be bottled and freeze-dried
perfect for dipping in your favorite dip
or adding texture to a casserole—

hold the money shot to the back of my head
and kiss me as you pull the trigger
the statement is true
and false
and everything in between
for the lifeboat
drifting empty
amid the ripples
of the sea.

THE MATARESE CIRCLE

"Very nice," said Scofield, meaning it, and her, and everything he saw.

"I feel like a traitor to all the things I've believed for so long," she added, whispering. "These prices could feed ten families for a month! Let's go somewhere else."

"We don't have time. Take them and get some kind of coat and anything else you need."

"You *are* mad."

"I'm in a hurry."

From a booth on the Via Sistina, he called a *pensione* in the Piazza Navona where he stayed frequently when in Rome. The landlord and his wife knew nothing at all about Scofield—they were not curious about any of their transient tenants—except that Bray tipped generously whenever they accommodated him. The owner was happy to do so tonight.

The Piazza Navona was crowded; it was always crowded, thus making it an ideal location for a man in his profession. The Bernini fountains were magnets for citizens and tourists alike, the profusion of outdoor cafes places of assignation, planned and spontaneous; Scofield's had always been planned. A table in a crowded square was a good vantage point for spotting surveillance. It was not necessary to be concerned about such things now.

Now it was only necessary to get some sleep, let the mind clear itself. Tomorrow a decision would have to be made. The life or the death of the woman at his side whom he guided through the Piazza to an old stone building and the door of the *pensione*.

The ceiling of their room was high, the windows enormous, opening onto the square three stories below. Bray pushed the overstuffed sofa against the door and pointed to the bed across the room.

"Neither of us slept very much on that damned boat. Get some rest."

Antonia opened one of the boxes from the shop in the Via Condotti and took out the dark silk dress. "Why did you buy me these expensive clothes?"

281

281
It's nice
yes it's all very nice
and the price is only
all you ever believed in
polishing the mirror
with an oily rag
squinting through the dusty window screen
with a highball in your hand
I say, open another bottle, what?
and if there's any ice left
bring it for my head—

how can I plan an assignation
with this body mangled in the war
the armored division was
inexorable as a tide
the farm girls in their attics
would give anything for an egg
or even an old turnip
but now it's time to get some sleep
let the mind clear
spit-shine it with that old rag
to keep the dreams away
if you grind enough dust
into the folds of your brain
you might feel you've come home
to touch the earth again
I tuck my crippled hand
in the lapel of my dinner jacket
one can almost ignore the pain
quite elegant, what?

anyway it's nice
it's always very nice
and the price is always
something you can pay
repose or dignity or something of the like
it's only ever one more thing
you have to find a way
to live without.

metal clattering against stone. Bray grabbed the man's throat, smashing his head into the wall, and twisting him by the neck into the open doorframe. He held the Italian upright, and hammered his fist into the man's lower rib cage; he could hear the bone crack. He plunged his knee into the small of the man's back and with both hands acting as a battering ram, sent him plummeting through the door into the room. The Italian collapsed over the obstructing sofa and fell senseless to the floor beyond it. Scofield turned and ran to Antonia.

Reaction was allowed now; he felt sick. Her face was bruised, spidery veins of red had spread from the swellings caused by repeated blows to the head. The corner of her left eye was so battered the skin had broken; a two-pronged rivulet of blood flowed down her cheek. The loose-fitting sweater had been removed by force, the white blouse torn to shreds, nothing left but ragged patches of fabric. Beneath, her brassiere had been pulled from its hasps, yanked off her breasts, hanging from a single shoulder strap.

It was the flesh of this exposed part of her body that made him swallow in revulsion. There were cigarette burns, ugly little circles of charred skin, progressing from her pelvic area across the flat of her stomach over the swell of her right breast toward the small red nipple.

The man who had done this to her was no interrogator seeking information; that role was secondary. He was a sadist, indulging his sickness as brutally and as rapidly as possible. And Bray had not finished with that man.

Antonia moaned, shaking her head back and forth, pleading not to be hurt again. He picked her up and carried her back into the room, kicking the door shut, edging his way around the sofa, past the unconscious man on the floor, to the bed. He placed her gently down, sat beside her and drew her to him.

"It's all right. It's over, he can't touch you anymore." He felt her tears against his face, and then was aware that she had put her arms around him. She was suddenly holding him fiercely, her body trembling, the cries from her throat more than pleas for

A palliative of violence
like a poultice spread across my skin
a bridle buckled to my head
a metal bit between my teeth
can't bite through can't spit it out
bones crack
and I sit in the sun wondering why
lines of ink don't unscroll from my hand
like they once did
some singing heart now paved with asphalt
as smoke rises to the sky—

he held the wine glass in a shaking hand
the hand that had caressed her throat
probing for weakness or desire
swallow your revulsion
along with everything else
the laminate glue that held us together
began eroding long ago
her memory still sucks to me like a kiss
though the dunes and bluffs of that summer
were razed to uniformity
making way for oil derricks and refinery towers—

another cup of coffee in the sun
maybe poetry will come back one day
like the spirit of an animal
extinct a hundred years
that hasn't given up hope yet.

THE MATARESE CIRCLE

Taleniekov looked up; the cryptographer spun in his chair. Twenty feet away, in an aisle peopled by waiters, were two men who had not come in for a meal; their expressions were set, their eyes darting about the room. They were scanning the tables but not for friends.

"Oh, my God," whispered the cryptographer, turning back to Vasili. "They found the phone and tapped it. I was afraid of that."

"Followed you, yes," said Taleniekov, glancing over at Zaimis, who was half out of his chair, the *idiot*. "They know we're friends; you're being watched. But they didn't find the phone. If they were certain that I was here, they'd break in with a dozen soldiers. They're district VKR. I know them. Calmly now, take off your hat and slide out of your chair. Head toward the back hallway, to the men's room. There's a rear exit, remember?"

"Yes, yes, I remember," sputtered the man. He got up, his shoulders hunched, and started for the narrow corridor several tables away.

But he was an academic, not a field man, and Vasili cursed himself for trying to instruct him. One of the two VKR men spotted him and came forward, pushing aside the waiters in the aisle.

Then he saw Taleniekov and his hand whipped into the open space of his jacket toward an unseen weapon. As he did so, the Greek seaman lurched up from his chair, weaving unsteadily, waving his arms like a man with too much vodka in him. He slammed against the VKR man, who tried to push him away. The Greek feigned drunken indignation and pushed back with such force that the Russian went sprawling over a table, sending dishes and food crashing to the floor.

Vasili sprang up and raced past his old friend from Riga, pulling him toward the narrow hallway; then he saw the American. Zaimis was on his feet, his gun in his hand. *Idiot!*

"Put that *away!*" shouted Taleniekov. "Don't expose—"

It was too late. A gunshot exploded through the sounds of chaos, escalating it instantly into pandemonium. The CIA man

105

105

I'm waiting for the Russian heiress
she's taking her time
busy with pearls and caviar I guess
while I'm stuck with the champagne bill
if I had an uzi in my guitar case
I could shoot or bluff my way out the back door
crooning don't pay for shit
but the cryptographer is never unemployed
he can crack any code except
why?

the Greek shared his bottle with the maître d'
they disappeared into the walk-in fridge
a pool of wine spread across the floor
I got down on my knees to drink
I had to push the dipsomaniac poodle away
I needed that red stain on my tongue
I needed my belly to turn to flowers
I needed hope to lie to me again
I needed lubrication to get through the day
or through the rear exit
maybe that's what the Russian heiress likes
she sent a note
inviting me to her penthouse suite
with a view across the river to the mountains
I told her I'm busy
who's got time for pretty pictures
for doormen and pedigree dogs
when the mystery is running through our fingers
disappearing before we have the chance to taste it
mopped up wrung out rinsed away
as if it had never been.

Scofield heard the footsteps in the hallway and got out of the chair. He walked to the door and peered through the tiny disk in the center. The figure of a man passed by; he did not stop at the door across the way, the entrance to the suite of rooms used by Taleniekov's courier. Bray went back to the chair and sat down. He leaned his head against the rim, staring at the ceiling.

It had been three days since the race in the streets, three nights since he'd taken the messenger from Taleniekov—messenger three nights ago, killer on the Unter den Linden ten years before. It had been a strange night, an odd race, a finish that might have been otherwise.

The man could have lived; the decision to kill him had gradually lost its urgency for Bray, as so much had lost urgency. The courier had brought it upon himself. The Soviet had gone into panic and pulled out a four-inch, razor-sharp blade from the recesses of the hotel chair and attacked. His death was due to Scofield's reaction; it was not the premeditated murder planned in the street.

Nothing ever changed much. The KGB courier had been used by Taleniekov. The man was convinced that Beowulf Agate was coming over, and the Russian who brought him in would be given the brassiest medal in Moscow.

"You've been tricked," Bray had told the courier.

"Impossible!" the Soviet had yelled. "It's Taleniekov!"

"It certainly is. And he chooses a man from the Unter den Linden to make contact, a man whose face he knows I'll never forget. The odds were that I'd lose control and kill you. In Washington. I'm exposed, vulnerable.... And you've been taken."

"You're wrong! It's a white contact!"

"So was East Berlin, you son of a bitch."

"What are you going to do?"

"Earn some of my severance pay. You're coming in."

"No!"

"Yes."

The man had lunged at Scofield.

Three days had passed since that moment of violence, three mornings since Scofield had deposited the package at the embassy

114

Don't tell me that son of a bitch
was ever in East Berlin
he was white slaving
in Caracas when INTERPOL picked him up that's all
drag-assing along on some
assassination team
El Cocodrilo ran out of Havana—

back at the central office
I always recognized his footsteps
striding down the hall to the shitter
everyone could
it was a matter of self-preservation
he tried to pull
that 4-inch blade
on every skirt in the mission
at one time or another
till the director
bought him a pet cat
thereafter feline vanity
was evident in the way he
twirled his moustache
and licked his lips in restaurants
the KGB courier
bribed him with filets mignon
and bourbon from duty free airport shops
he was the blandest fish in the school—

the night he got burned
the rain came down like plastic mulch
emptied from the sky
headlights came probing through like tongues
El Cocodrilo always had a light touch
but he fucked the pooch that time
a single pay phone call
was all it took
no one will ever know if it was a mistake
or an order from above—

he got the full
severance package of course
they always tie off the bag
when they throw out the scraps
to keep them from the rats
even the wharf thugs know
how to read between the lines.

THE MATARESE CIRCLE

and sent the cipher to Sevastopol. Still no one had come to the door across the hall; and that was not normal. The suite was leased by a brokerage house in Bern, Switzerland, to be available for its "executives." Standard procedure for international businessmen, and also a transparent cover for a Soviet drop.

Bray had forced the issue. The cipher and the courier's dead body *had* to provoke someone into checking the suite of rooms. Yet no one had; it did not make sense.

Unless part of Taleniekov's cable was true: he *was* acting alone. If that were the case, there was only one explanation: the Soviet killer had been terminated, and before retiring to an isolated life somewhere in the vicinity of Grasnov, he had decided to settle an outstanding debt.

He had sworn to do so after Prague; the message had been clear: *You're mine, Beowulf Agate. Someday, somewhere. I'll see you take your last breath.*

A brother for a wife. The husband for the brother. It was vengeance rooted in loathing and that loathing never left. There'd be no peace for either of them until the end came for one. It was better to know that now, thought Bray, rather than find out on a crowded street or a deserted stretch of beach, with a knife in the side or a bullet in the head.

The courier's death was an accident, Taleniekov's would not be. There *would* be no peace until they met, and then death would come—one way or the other. It was a question now of drawing the Russian out; he had made the first move. He was the stalker, the role established.

The strategy was classic: tracks clearly defined for the stalker to follow, and at the chosen moment—least expected—the tracks would not be there, the stalker bewildered, exposed—the trap sprung.

Like Bray, Taleniekov could travel anywhere he wished, with or without official sanction. Over the years, both had learned too many methods; a plethora of false papers were out there for purchase, hundreds of men everywhere ready to provide concealment or transportation, cover or weapons—any and all. There

115

115
When he ascended to the premiership,
his first act was to have the nuclear codes
tattooed onto his penis. Due to incompetence
or elements of dissent within the administration
his staff did not inform him that the codes
were automatically reconfigured every 6 hours
via heavily encrypted random generation
algorithms. He was furious when
he woke the next day to learn he had nothing
but lines of obsolete gibberish embossed
into his most sensitive extremity, still
smarting from the needle. The illusion of
his country's self-determination was shattered
when he ordered the nuclear codes to be
permanently set to the ones he had
entrusted to his "right hand man,"
as he referred to the appendage in question,
and was informed that the nation's "benefactors"
would never acquiesce to so flaccid
an approximation of security. For the next month
he devoted the resources of his office to researching
the modification of subdermally embedded ink,
but was told even the most advanced
laser technology would render his beloved
deputy as a neutered stick of
scar tissue after only a few erasures
and re-writings.

                In a rage, he bellowed
in that case he would immediately
launch the full nuclear arsenal, wherever
it might be aimed, to enshrine the apotheosized digits
in an eternal posterity of annihilation.
With a savage unzipping
that according to witnesses included
the sound of tearing flesh,
he brought forth the
"right hand man" to provide the codes. Fortunately
the writing surface in question was so

distorted by tumescence that the symbols were illegible—
thus, in the Western media's account of events,
nuclear armageddon was averted. Of course,
at the moment he exposed himself
the codes were long outdated anyway.

THE MATARESE CIRCLE

unsteady. He kept checking his watch, the light too dim for his eyes; he was jostled by pedestrians whenever he stopped. And he stopped incessantly, breath and strength diminishing. Twice he started for an omnibus shelter in the block beyond where he stood, momentarily convinced that he had made the wrong count of the streets; at the intersection where the Kirov Theatre stood, there were three shelters and his confusion mounted. He visited all three, more and more bewildered.

The strategy had the expected effect on the woman following Mikovsky. She interpreted the old man's actions as those of a subject aware that he might be under surveillance, a subject unschooled in methods of evasion but also old and frightened and capable of creating an uncontrollable situation. So the woman in the brown overcoat and visored cap kept her distance, staying in shadows, going from darkened storefront to dimly lit alleyways, propelled into agitation herself by the unpredictability of her subject.

The old scholar started on his return pattern to the library. Vasili and Maletkin watched from a vantage point, seventy-five meters away. Taleniekov studied the route directly across the wide avenue; there were two alleyways, both of which would be used by the woman as Mikovsky passed her on the way back.

"Come along," ordered Vasili, grabbing Maletkin's arm, pushing him forward. "We'll get behind him in the crowd on the other side. She'll turn away as he goes by, and when he passes that second alleyway, she'll use it."

"Why are you so sure?"

"Because she used it before; it's the natural thing to do. I'd use it. We will use it now."

"How?"

"I'll tell you when we're in position."

The moment was drawing near and Taleniekov could feel the drumlike beat in his chest. He had orchestrated the events of the past sixteen minutes, the next few would determine whether the orchestration had merit. He knew two indisputable facts: one, the woman would recognize him instantly; she would have been

365

365

The project was initially code-named HIROSHIMA
but this was soon changed to PAVLOV
in some cynical concession to tact.
The flood of propaganda unloosed upon
supposedly allied populations
was so incessant and unrelenting
that field agents referred to the program as DIARRHEA,
but as disaffection spread implacably
through the ranks they further lampooned
it as THE MOVEMENT.
Despite the heroic historical terms
in which THE MOVEMENT had been presented
in its fiscal budget proposal,
it accomplished little
except a roiling general confusion, a chain
reaction of psychic entropy which likely
served the centers of power as well as or better than
the stated aims of the mission.
Incompetence and wrong moves came to define
THE MOVEMENT to the point that no one on the
ground had loyalty to anything but saving his own ass,
again probably more effective for its agendas
than solidarity to a common code.

When the lot fell to me to carry out the latest
haphazard and ill-conceived assassination,
I decided to defect, but no longer knew which side
I was on. My handler gave me a vial of radioactive poison
and a description of a target so vague and self-
contradictory
it could have been a person
of any race, gender, height or weight,
political belief or sexual predilection.
I steered the black agency sedan
to the frontier then
traded it to an inbred dwarf
for a shitty rusted compact.
I filled the tank and drove till it was empty.
I taped the vial of poison

to the skin above my heart
and started walking into the tundra,
Alaska or Siberia
I wasn't sure which.
My steps were pleasantly springy on the moss
and the melting permafrost beneath.
I wondered if anyone was following me,
and whether wild animals or the radiation
would catch me first.

Communist killer? Where's the verification, even the logic? Goddamn it, we're cut off. All we've got are shadows!"

Taleniekov took a step forward, his conviction in his voice. "Perhaps old Krupskaya was right; perhaps the answer is in Corsica after all."

"Oh, Christ."

"Hear me out. You say we have only shadows. If so we need a great deal more. If we *had* more, traced even a few names, constructed a fabric of probability—built our own case, if you will. Then could you go to someone, force him to listen to you?"

"From a distance," answered Bray slowly. "Only from a distance. Beyond reach."

"Naturally."

"The case would have to be more than probable, it'd have to be damned conclusive."

"I could move men in Moscow if I had such proof. It was my hope that over here an inquiry might be made with less evidence. You're notorious for your never-ending Senate inquiries. I merely assumed it could be done, that you could bring it about."

"Not now. Not me."

"Corsica, then?"

"I don't know. I'd have to think about it. There's still Winthrop."

"You said yourself you could not reach him. If you tried to get near him, they'd kill you."

"People have tried before. I'll protect myself. I've got to find out what happened. He saw it for himself; if he's alive and I can talk to him, he'll know what to do."

"And if he's *not* alive, or you cannot reach him?"

Scofield looked at the dead men on the pavement. "Maybe the only thing that's left. Corsica."

The KGB man shook his head. "I look at odds more thoroughly than you, Beowulf. I won't wait. I won't risk that hospital you speak of. I'll go to Corsica now."

"If you do, start on the southeast coast, north of Porto Vecchio."

"Why?"

"It's where it all began. It's Matarese country."

195

195
Armed men stormed the town square
and fired their weapons at the sky.
They leaned against the colonial arches
of flaking ocher paint
and scuffed their boots on the cobblestones,
smoking corn husk cigarettes
and looking blankly at the empty streets.

Mafia killer can be two things
with opposite meanings,
but as the shadows of afternoon
drew across the bandstand and the tree-lined plaza,
and the women selling fruit and flowers
remained behind locked doors,
the distinction seemed gratuitous, even ridiculous,
since all guns are made to fire bullets into bodies,
hitmen and soldiers are hired
to pull triggers to protect or kill,
but allegiances and principles
wash out in the end,
leaving residues of waste and grief.

I sat in the cantina
drinking rum and coffee
waiting to see if the mayor's men would counterattack
but by dusk everyone was hungry
no insurrection yet has defeated a grumbling belly
even if it starts with one.
The Maoist rebels or narco-mercenaries,
whichever they were,
melted out of sight
and reappeared at the cantina door,
balaclavas stuffed in their pockets,
weapons half-concealed in their coats,
asking for coffee and tortillas,
apologizing in advance they couldn't pay.

In the light of a kerosene lamp
they talked of seasons and fields

of horses and oxen
the limitless acreage of the fincas
and the wealth and cruelty of the bosses.
Each man shared his view
of when the war would end
the war of brother on brother
farmer on farmer
and each nodded as the others spoke
as if in favor of
any future that was not
an endless extension of the present,
endorsing an allegiance
with the gods of chance and change
to accept whatever they might bring,
an end and a beginning,
the pain and possibility
of all that's left to come.

THE MATARESE CIRCLE

MATARSE CIRCULO

Pietre Maletkin stood next to Vasili in the shadows of an archway across from the southeast entrance to the Saltykov-Shchedrin Library. The floodlights in the rear courtyard of the complex shone down in wide circles from the high walls, giving the illusion of an enormous prison compound. But the arches that led to the street beyond were placed symmetrically every hundred feet in the wall; the prisoners could come and go at will. It was a busy evening at the library; streams of prisoners came and went.

"You say this old man is one of us?" asked Maletkin.

"Get your new enemies straight, comrade. The old fellow's KGB, the man following him—about to make contact—is one of us. We've got to reach him before he's trapped. The scholar is one of the most effective weapons Moscow's developed for counterintelligence. His name is known to no more than five people in KGB; to be aware of him marks a person as an American informer. For God's sake, don't ever mention him."

"I've never heard of him," said Maletkin. "But the Americans think he's *theirs*?"

"Yes. He's a plant. He reports everything directly to Moscow on a private line."

"Incredible," muttered the traitor. "An old man. Ingenious."

"My former associates are not fools," said Taleniekov, checking his watch. "Neither are your present ones. Forget you've ever heard of Comrade Mikovsky."

"That's his name?"

"Even I would rather not repeat it. . . . There he is."

An old man bundled up in an overcoat and a black fur hat walked out of the entrance, his breath vaporizing in the cold air. He stood for a moment on the steps, looking around as if trying to decide which archway to take into the street. His short beard was white, what could be seen of his face was filled with wrinkles and tired, pale flesh. He started down the stairs cautiously, holding on to the railing. He reached the courtyard and walked toward the nearest arch on his right.

Taleniekov studied the stream of people that came out through the glass doors after the old curator. They seemed to be in groups

363
Armed men occupied the central market.
Rebel insignia were sewn onto their ruined
coats, but in a haphazard manner
more like a bad pastiche of insurrection
than the stern, disciplined reputation of
the guerilla army in the hills. Was this a sloppy bit of
false flag theater by the government,
grist for the propaganda mill,
or something dreamed up to break the tedium of official
life?
Or could it have been
rebels masquerading as the army imitating rebels,
acting out a farce as imposters of themselves?
No one would likely ever know, not even
the men themselves.

They were thin and dirty
and held their AKs and 16s like evil talismans,
poison snakes or pails of human waste—
weapons left over from the regional proxy wars,
passed hand to hand for decades between men,
between causes and armies,
their black finish worn to a metal gleam,
the wooden stocks of the older rifles
blanched and cracked. There was of course
not the faintest hint of a police presence
during the hours of the occupation.
The women and girls of the market watched the
proceedings blankly, as if sitting through an all-night
indoctrination session,
waiting for the slurry of ideology to pass
so the current of life could resume again.

At a sign from a bearded man
wearing pressed fatigues and sunglasses,
the men raised their weapons and fired
into the sky, astonished
as the bursts of automatic fire echoed off the
metal doors of the warehouse bays.

After a half-hearted raised-fist salute
the men climbed in their
pickups and drove away, looking back
at the charcoal fires the women were already relighting
beneath their rows of roasting corn.

Down the hill behind the market,
a wooden bridge spanned a stream
black with toxic runoff from the dump,
to a settlement of indigenous dwellings
made from plywood, old tires, and plastic scraps.
At the moment the men
released their aimless volley
at the sky, a young girl
was carrying her baby brother
across the bridge in a cotton sling,
heading home, wearing an
embroidered skirt and taffeta blouse.
One of the bullets,
returning to earth,
descended past her collarbone
into her ribcage
and exploded her heart.
As she crumpled
to the walkway
she shielded the infant
with her body
as she fell.

no inkling that there was a shred of credibility to what he said."

There was a pause. "I called my guard, told the American to remain where he was. He is under the gun, still by the fountain."

"You *what*? You left him with a *guard*? An *American*? Are you mad? That is impossible. He is no such thing!"

"He's American, of course he is! His English is American—completely American. He uses the name Pastor, I told you that!"

Another pause, this one ominous, the tension electric. "You were always the weakest link, Guillamo; we know that. But now you've caved in too far. You've left an open question where there can be *none*! That man is Vasili Taleniekov! He changes languages as a chameleon alters its colors, and he will kill a guard with no more effort than stepping on a maggot. We cannot afford you, Guillamo. There can be no link at all. None whatsoever."

Silence . . . brief, cut short by a gunshot and a gutteral explosion of breath. Guillamo Scozzi was dead.

"Leave him!" commanded the unknown *consigliere* of the Matarese. "He'll be found in the morning, his car at the bottom of the gorge of Hadrian. Go find this Pastor, this elusive Taleniekov! He won't be taken alive, don't try. Find him. Kill him. . . . And the girl in white. She, also. Kill them both."

Scofield lunged down the narrow staircase, around the curve. The last words he heard from beyond the door above, however, were so strange, so arresting, he nearly stopped, tempted to fire at the emerging killers and go back up to face the unknown man, who spoke them.

". . . *Scozzi*! Mother of Christ! Reach Turin. Tell them to cable the eagles, the cat. The burials must be absolute."

There was no time to think, he had to reach Antonia; he had to get them out of Villa d'Este. He pulled back the door and rushed out into the pounding madness. Suddenly, he was aware of the row of chairs lined up against the wall; most were empty, some draped with discarded capes and furs and stoles.

If he could eliminate one pursuer the advantage would be several fold. One man sending out an alarm would be far less effective than two. And there was something else. A trapped man convinced he was about to lose his life would more than likely reveal

331

331
I was talking to myself again.
This was nothing new, but
now it was different, I couldn't stop,
as if my volition were displaced
by a perpetual motion machine,
an engine imposed from beyond myself
to run on nerves and blood.
The sun dragged through the dust
of the plaza like a bootheel. With my tongue
I caressed my cyanide tooth, the left
upper canine—but
I couldn't remember if it was really
deadly poison or if my handlers had implanted
erectile dysfunction medication in my skull instead.
Assassins watched me from café tables
concealing revolvers with newspapers,
camouflaging themselves with flowered shirts
amid the sprays of plastic flowers.

Death or virility, each is its own transcendence,
its own contortion, its own
form of tender violence.
When you talk to
yourself is anyone listening?
I tried to lend an ear to myself,
and decided to visit the Hotel Tivoli
with its sad girls
and sadder accordion players. I would
drink a beer, banter with the matron, then
bite through my fake truth, I mean tooth,
succumb to the chemical it contained and
to its fate, either way it would be
ecstasy and release
and the voices I couldn't stop
would at last subside
like shadows
at the bottom of a well
abiding
inside me.

ROBERT LUDLUM
MATARSE CIRCULO

"I think you skipped something," interrupted Bray again. "I assume that was when you said you were me."

"Let's say I answered in the affirmative when the hysterical question was posed. It was a temptation I could not resist, since I had heard less than forty-eight hours previously that you had been killed." The Russian paused, then added, "Two weeks ago in Washington."

Scofield walked back to the chair, frowning. "But the man on the phone knew I was alive, just as those here in London knew I was alive. So you were right. Only certain people inside the Matarese were told I was dead."

"Does that tell you something?"

"The same thing it tells you. They make distinctions."

"Exactly. When either of us ever wanted a subordinate to do nothing, we told him the problem was solved. For such people you're no longer alive, no longer hunted."

"But why? I *am* hunted. They trapped me."

"One question with two answers, I think," said the Russian. "As any diverse organization, the Matarese is imperfect. Among its ranks are the undisciplined, the violence-prone, men who kill for the score alone or because of fanatic beliefs. These were the people who were told you were dead. If they did not hunt you, they would not kill you."

"That's your first answer; what's the second? Why does someone want to keep me alive?"

"To make you a *consigliere* of the Matarese."

"What?"

"Think about it. Consider what you'd bring to such an organization."

Bray stared at the KGB man. "No more than you would."

"Oh, much more. There are no great shocks to come out of Moscow, I accept that. But there are astonishing revelations to be found in Washington. You could provide them; you'd be an enormous asset. The sanctimonious are always far more vulnerable."

"I accept that."

"Before Odile Verachten was killed, she made an offer to me. It

466

466

The regimes demand and accept nothing
but subordination. When after several decades of fealty
I could no longer comply, they declared me
dead—murder or suicide, the ambiguity
was allowed to swirl. I remained in London,
no longer hunted, but simply disregarded.
Skip to my Lou, my darling, through
the tourist crowds of Trafalgar Square
or along the old wharfs of the Isle of Dogs,
no passport, no contingency plan, just the ghost
of wetlands buried by pavement and
a sift of history like powdered sugar on blancmange.
The KGB stayed as far from me as my
ostensible former masters. I became a
relic of my own solitude, useless as
a rotted fish floating on the surface
of a current. I pawned my Mauser and my
Glock. I got my teeth fixed and replaced my glass eye
with one that was bloodshot and dilated.
I bought bones from the butchers and
tossed them to the strays as I covered the waterfront.

Despite my dereliction, someone wanted me alive—
every few months I returned from my perambulations
to find an envelope of notes on the bedstand of my room
at the Tivoli Hotel, with its eternal
smell of dirty sheets and kidney pies.
My old handler used to call me a
sanctimonious son of a bitch, then
we'd laugh and toss back a dram of single-malt.
Now, as the new war was announced in the papers—
really just an iteration of the old war that had never
ceased—
he showed up at my door and offered me a post in Kiev.
It was rehabilitation as a means of termination, as he
made clear.
I accepted without protest. I missed the taste of borscht
and remembered a Bulgarian dulcimer player
I once knew in Odesa. If I found her,
we could make a run for Varna
and walk along the shore, holding hands,
the Black Sea lapping at our feet.

was not an offer she was entitled to make; they don't want the Russian. They want you. If they can't have you, they'll kill you, but someone's giving you the option."

It would be far better for all concerned if we sat down and thrashed out the differences between us. You may discover they're not so great after all. Words from a faceless messenger.

"Let's get back to Paris," said Bray. "How did you get her?"

"It wasn't so difficult. The man on the phone was too anxious; he saw a generalship in his future, or his own execution. I discussed what might happen to the soldier with the ugly little mark on his chest; the fact that I knew about it was nearly enough in itself. I set up a series of moves, offering the soldier and Beowulf Agate for the girl. Beowulf was tired of running and was perfectly willing to listen to whatever anyone had to say. He—I—knew I was cornered, but professionalism demanded that he—you— extract certain guarantees. The girl had to go free. Were my reactions consistent with your well-known obstinacy?"

"Very plausible," replied Scofield. "Let's see if I can fill in a few spaces. You answered the questions: What was my mother's middle name? or When did my father change jobs?"

"Nothing so ordinary," broke in the Russian. "Who was your fourth kill? Where?"

"Lisbon," said Bray quietly. "An American beyond salvage. Yes, you'd know that. Then your moves were made by a sequence of telephone calls to the flat—my call from London was the intrusion—and with each call you gave new instructions, any deviation and the exchange was canceled. The exchange ground itself was in traffic, preferably one-way traffic, with one vehicle, one man and Antonia. Everything to take place within a time span of sixty to a hundred seconds."

The Russian nodded. "Noon on the Champs Elysées, south of the Arch. Vehicle and girl taken, man and soldier bound at the elbows, thrown out at the intersection of the Place de la Concorde, and a swift, if roundabout, drive out of Paris."

Bray put the whisky down, and walked to the hotel window overlooking Carlos Place. "A little while ago you said you had two choices. To go out after her, or wait in the rue de Bac. It seems to

467

467

We bound the soldier at the elbows and
threw him off the train at Gare du Nord.
It was a salvage mission beyond salvage, bartering ruin
for expired promises. Men in white suits
used to mean the funny farm—
now they come in full hazmat gear,
carry assault rifles instead of straightjackets,
and you'll be on the run
for a long time to come.

Every empire is a salvage economy,
every war is a resource war.
Every capital has its Arc de Triomphe
made from bayonets of fallen soldiers
powdered bones are mixed with cement
at the heart of the great metropolis grids.
And the empire itself is beyond salvage,
recycling bullet casings into tourist trinkets
that are sold, discarded, melted down
and poured into molds again
for the latest fashionable cause.

100 seconds
for nuclear warheads to span the sea.

I staggered down the Champs Élysées
drunk on *vin rouge* from a tetrapak,
eating a cheeseburger and fries,
my armpits reeking of burnt onions
and dead roses. The gendarmes were disgusted
as they watched me with their slick haircuts and
perfectly razored beards, holding high-caliber
weapons in their arms like post-coital lovers.

I didn't care.
By this time my sense of self was like a set of
antique tennis gear—
animal gut, warped and splintered wood
and a pair of sad, deflated balls.

I turned and watched a garbage scow
floating down the Seine. Beyond it
the Eiffel Tower was a bayonet of girders
stabbing at the sky.

The gendarmes pinned my arms behind my back
and bound my elbows. One offered me a cigarette
held a Zippo to my lips, and said,
We'll give you two choices,
but there's nowhere you can go.
All throughout the war
but we never really wanted the Russians,
we only wanted you.

THE MATARESE CIRCLE

"It never died out. It went further underground—became dormant, if you like—but it returned in a far more dangerous form. It's been operating since the early fifties. It operates now. It has infiltrated the most sensitive and powerful areas of both our governments. Its objective is the control over both our countries. The Matarese was responsible for the murders of General Blackburn here and Dimitri Yurievich in my country."

Bray sipped his coffee, studying the Russian's face over the rim of the cup. "How do you know that? Why do you believe it?"

"An old man who saw more in his lifetime than you and I combined, made the identification. He was not wrong; he was one of the few who admitted—or will ever admit—having dealt with the Matarese."

"*Saw? Was?* Past tenses."

"He died. He called for me while he was dying; he wanted me to know. He had access to information neither you nor I would be given under any circumstances."

"Who was he?"

"Aleksie Krupskaya. The name is meaningless, I realize, so I'll explain."

"Meaningless?" interrupted Scofield, crossing to an armchair in front of the fire, and sitting down. "Not entirely. Krupskaya, the white cat of Krivoi Rog. Istrebiteli. The last of the exterminators from Section Nine, KGB. The original Nine, of course."

"You do your schoolwork well, but then, as they say, you're a Harvard man."

"That kind of schoolwork can be helpful. Krupskaya was banished twenty years ago. He became a nonperson. If he were alive, I figured he was vegetating in Grasnov, not a consultant being fed information by people in the Kremlin. I don't believe your story."

"Believe it now," said Talemekov, sitting down opposite Bray. "Because it was not *people* in the Kremlin, just one man. His son. For thirty years one of the highest-ranking survivors of the Politburo. For the past six, Premier of Soviet Russia."

Scofield put his cup down on the floor and again studied the KGB man's face. It was the face of a practiced liar, a professional

179

179
I was recruited to an entry level position as a career perjurer.
The appointment included the benefits and staggered promotion schedule
commensurate with the prestige of a global corporate regime.
A hired assassin can never be sure if his target
or he himself is innocent—likewise I never again knew
if words programmed to emerge from my mouth were
true or false, life-saving or -destroying.

From the moment my training and facial mechanization
were complete, life existed in the past tense,
as if everything had happened already,
every possibility foretold,
reduced to a standard format and filed in advance.
My connection to a present organic reality dissolved,
and with it every trace of passion, compassion,
ingenuity, sensuality, pain—all that feels and breathes
in a living moment became obsolete,
displaced by algorithms,
a script fixed, fait accompli or fabricated,
though no less unalterable for that.

If language defines reality then lies can
determine truth. My body became a shell
with no function but to manifest
a paradigm, every cell and pore
colonized by a status quo I could no longer
distinguish from myself. I had access to
information I never knew existed, but in order to
share it in any form of dissent or revelation
I would have had to sever an arm, gouge loose an eye,
carve out a kidney, or hack off my genitals.
And who might thus receive them? Everyone's
perception was similarly circumscribed,
flesh and blood compending to internecine certainties.

Believe me, I pleaded with my eyes

when I was caught behind the shifting lines
of the information war. But my interrogators,
whichever side they were on,
had been remade into vessels for automated narratives,
just like me.
A glass wall stood between us.
We looked at each other with open mouths
as white noise eddied from the two-way speaker,

as the polygraph hummed
and traced the mountain range of my pulse neon green
against the black glow of a screen.
None of us
could speak a single word.

THE MATARESE CIRCLE

"Easily dispatched and recorded." Taleniekov pushed himself away from the desk, his every instinct telling him he was near the truth. "What better way for a man like Voroshin to lose his identity but in the chaos of a revolution? The mobs out of control; the discipline did not come for weeks, and it was a miracle it came then. Absolute chaos. How easily it could be done."

"You're oversimplifying," said Mikovsky. "Although there was a period of rampage, teams of observers traveled throughout the cities and countryside writing down everything they saw and heard. Not only facts but impressions, opinions, interpretations of what they witnessed. The academicians insisted upon it, for it was a moment in history that would never be repeated and they wanted no instant lost, none unaccounted for. Everything was written down, no matter how harsh the observation. *That* was a form of discipline, Vasili."

Taleniekov nodded. "Why do you think I'm here?"

The old man sat forward. "The archives of the revolution?"

"I must see them."

"An easy request to make but most difficult to grant. The authority must come from Moscow."

"How is it relayed?"

"Through the Ministry of Cultural Affairs. A man is sent over from the Leningrad office with the key to the rooms below. There is no key here."

Vasili's eyes strayed to the mounds of papers on Mikovsky's desk. "Is that man an archivist? A scholar such as yourself?"

"No. He is merely a man with a key."

"How often are the authorizations granted?"

Mikovsky frowned. "Not very frequently. Perhaps twice a month."

"When was the last time?"

"About three weeks ago. An historian from the Zhdanov doing research."

"Where did he do his reading?"

"In the archive rooms. Nothing is permitted to be taken from them."

Taleniekov held up his hand. "Something was. It was sent to

377

377
"Horses or bulls?" I asked.
I tried to keep the irony from my voice,
but it was a bit of a tired joke, everyone knew
they'd all be slaughtered by the end
of the afternoon. The arena smelled of
marigolds and urine, dust coated
our eyes and teeth. My bowtie
choked my throat like an evil hand.
"What about the men," she asked,
twirling her tangerine parasol, sweat and pearls
glistening in the hollow of her throat.
"No need to worry about them," I said,
"in a few hours they'll be powdered and shaved,
drinking brandy with a meal of T-bones and rib eyes,
receiving sycophantic praise for their
heroic efforts, not a spot of blood
in their brilliantined mustachios."

She looked down at the rose petal floating
in her champagne glass and said,
"Your carnation has wilted in the heat."
"I know, it does so every time." I didn't
even need to check.
                         The archives
of the revolution were written in our
bodies, but was there anyone left to
read them?
                  The national anthem
crackled and blared from the public address
system. We stood up into the sun bashing down
like planks of raw lumber. The men and
animals were paraded in to begin the pageant.
The matador strutted like Chanticleer,
caressing his gilt-handled sword, brocade
glinting on the bulge of his groin.
The horses pranced nervously, the bull in his chute
twitched his withers,
the hump of gristle and bone impotent
against a maddening swarm of flies.

Of course, such spectacles have become
quite common to us by now, we only
attended at the ambassador's insistence.
A pubescent boy played a bugle out of tune
to signal the start of the ritual, the crowd
threw their cups into the air, a mist of beer
drifted golden on the breeze.
"Let's go to the dog fights next time," she said,
"they're less civilized but so much more honest."
I gave her the linen handkerchief from my breast pocket,
she dabbed the sweat and beer spray from her lips.

THE MATARESE CIRCLE

Voroshin-Verachten. Dead.

Sacrificed.

The direct descendants were expendable, which meant they were not the true inheritors of the Corsican *padrone*. They had been merely messengers, bearing gifts for others far more powerful, far more capable of spreading the Corsican fever.

This world needs killers?

To save it from killers! Odile Verachten had said.

Enigma.

David Waverly, Foreign Secretary, Great Britain.

Joshua Appleton, IV, Senator, United States Congress.

Were they, too, expendable messengers? Or were they something else? Did each carry the mark of the jagged blue circle on his chest? Had Scozzi? And if either did, or Scozzi had, was that unnatural blemish the mark of mystical distinction Odile Verachten had thought it was, or was it, too, something else? A symbol of expendability, perhaps. For it occurred to Vasili that wherever that mark appeared, death was a partner.

Scofield was searching in England now. The same Beowulf Agate that someone within the Matarese had reported killed in Rock Creek Park. Who was that someone, and why had the false report gone out? It was as though that person—or persons—wanted Scofield spared, beyond reach of the Matarese killers. But why?

You talk of the shepherd. He knows! Can you doubt it?

The shepherd. A shepherd boy.

Enigma.

Taleniekov put the tea down on the tray in front of him, his elbow jarred by his seat companion. The businessman from Essen had fallen asleep, his arm protruding over the divider. Vasili was about to remove it when his eyes fell on the folded newspaper spread out on the German's lap.

The photograph stared up at him and he stopped breathing, sharp bolts of pain returning to his chest.

The smiling, gentle face was that of Heinrich Kassel. The bold print above the photograph screamed the information.

* * *

427

427
They found the poet's body
covered in his own shit
in the shower stall of a room
in the Caracas red light district.
He had traveled south through the Darien Gap,
the opposite direction of the migrants
seeking asylum from the resource wars
that never ended in their homes.
The bedsheets were stained with semen
and tears from someone whose DNA
did not match his.
A Washington DC phone number
was written on a mirror in lipstick,
and on the cracked tile floor
lay an empty vodka bottle
and a copy of *Die Zeit*
open to a soft profile of the poet
with a grainy portrait
on which was scrawled in ballpoint ink
poetry is an antiviral virus.
His final poem in an otherwise empty notebook said

> the flow of money
> controls the flow of love
> and must flow down

> I was always a migrant
> but I never arrived
> except to the understanding
> there's no place left to go.

THE MATARESE CIRCLE

Taleniekov breathed deeply before answering. "They killed in Leningrad, in Essen," he said, his voice barely audible. "Oh, how they kill, these twentieth-century *Fida'is*, these contemporary mutants of Hasan ibn-al-Sabbah. I should tell you, the soldier I pushed from the car in the Place de la Concorde had more than a blemish on his chest. His clothes were stained by a gunshot that left another mark. I told his associate it was for Leningrad, for Essen."

The Russian told his story quietly, the depth of his feelings apparent when he spoke of Lodzia Kronescha, the scholar Mikovsky, and Heinrich Kassel. Especially Lodzia; it was necessary for him to stop for a while and pour more whisky in his glass. Scofield remained silent; there was nothing he could say. The Russian finished with the field at night in Stadtwald and the death of Odile Verachten.

"Prince Andrei Voroshin became Ansel Verachten, founder of the Verachten Works, next to Krupp the largest company in Germany, now one of the most sprawling in all Europe. The granddaughter was his chosen successor in the Matarese."

"And Scozzi," said Bray, "joined Paravacini through a marriage of convenience. Bloodlines, a certain talent, and charm in exchange for a seat in the board room. But the chair was a prop; it's all it ever was. The count was expendable, killed because he made a mistake."

"As was Odile Verachten. Also expendable."

"And the name Scozzi-Paravacini is misleading. The control lies with Paravacini."

"Add to that Trans-Communication's ownership of Verachten. So two descendants of the *padrone*'s guest list are accounted for, both a part of Matarese, yet neither significant. What do we have?"

"What we suspected, what old Krupskaya told you in Moscow. The Matarese was taken over, obviously in part, possibly in whole. Scozzi and Voroshin were useful for what they brought or what they knew or what they owned. They were tolerated—even made to feel important—as long as they *were* useful, eliminated the moment they were not."

"But useful for *what?* That's the question!" Taleniekov banged

469
"But useful for *what*?"

PART II

THE MATARESE CIRCLE

"Paravacini."

Bray viced a last clamp on the killer's windpipe; the air to the lungs and the head was suspended for slightly more than two seconds; the man fell limp. Scofield angled him down over the adjacent chair, one more drunken *bello Romano*.

He turned and threaded his way through the narrow path between the row of chairs and the jagged line of fever-pitched dancers. The first man had gone outside; Bray could roam freely for a minute or two, but no longer. He pressed his way through the crowd in the entranceway and walked into a less-frenzied gathering in the next room.

He saw her in the corner, the dark-haired Paolo standing next to her, two other *cavalieri* in front, all vying for her attention. Paolo, however, seemed less insistent; he knew future possessions when he saw them, where his count was concerned. The first thought that came to Bray's mind was that Toni's dress had to be covered.

... *the girl in white. She, also, kill them both.* ...

He walked rapidly up to the foursome, knowing precisely what he would do. A diversion was needed, the more hysterical the better. He touched Paolo's arm, his eyes on Antonia, his look telling her to stay quiet.

"You *are* Paolo, aren't you?" he asked the dark-haired man in Italian.

"Yes, sir."

"Count Guillamo wants to see you right away. It's some kind of emergency, I think."

"Of course! Where is he, sir?"

"Go through the arch over there and turn right, past a row of chairs, to a door. There's a staircase. ..." The young Italian rushed away; Bray excused Toni and himself from the remaining two men. He held her arm and propelled her toward the arch that led into the disco.

"What's happening?" she asked.

"We're leaving," he answered. "Inside here, there are some coats and things on the chairs. Grab the darkest and the largest one you can find. Quickly, we haven't much time."

She found a long black cape, as Bray stood between her and the

333

333
clamp
air to your lungs
breathe
the jagged line of dancers
in your body
too long
captive
pedestrians in the
mechanical street

insistent future possessions
had to be covered
like collateral
for some outlandish wager
on a roll of loaded dice

but stay quiet
butterflies will alight
on the rim of your champagne glass
right away
the effervescence fades

there's a staircase
leading to the disco
she found a long black cape
to wrap around her voice
the villa wall is topped
with honeysuckle and razor wire
the hummingbirds
with pulsing iridescent throats
watch you as they
come and go.

THE MATARESE CIRCLE

"*Christ*. . ." uttered Scofield softly. *All of us*. They were legion. Girls taken from the camps, sent to the war fronts, to barracks everywhere, to airfields. Surviving as whores, dishonored by their own, unwanted, ostracized. They became the scavengers of Europe. Taleniekov *did* know where to find his flocks.

"Why do you work for him? He's no better than those who sent you to the camps."

"I have to. He'll kill me. Now you say you will."

"Thirty seconds ago, I would have. You didn't give me a choice; you can now. I'll take care of you. You stay in contact with this man. How?"

"He calls. In the suite across the hall."

"How often."

"Every ten or fifteen minutes. He'll call again soon."

"Let's go," said Bray cautiously. "Move to your right and drop the knife on the bed."

"Then you'll *shoot*," whispered the old woman.

"If I was going to, I'd do it now," said Scofield. He *needed* her, needed her confidence. "There'd be no reason to wait, would there? Let's get over to that phone. Whatever he was paying, I'll double."

"I don't think I can walk. I think you broke my foot."

"I'll help you." Bray lowered the towel and took a step toward her. He held out his hand. "Take my arm."

The old woman placed her left foot in front of her painfully. Then suddenly, like an enraged lioness, she lunged forward, her face again contorted, her eyes wild.

The blade came rushing toward Scofield's stomach.

Taleniekov followed the man from Amsterdam into the elevator. There was one other couple in the car. Young, rich, pampered Americans; fashionably dressed lovers or newlyweds, aware only of themselves and their hungers. They had been drinking.

The Hollander in the black overcoat removed his gray homburg, as Vasili, his face briefly turned away, stood next to him against the paneled wall of the small enclosure. The doors closed. The girl laughed softly; her companion pressed the button for the fifth

147

147
Christ
had nothing to sell the
girls
surviving as whores
scavengers
in a wasteland of
pubic hair and paper scraps
I'll take care of you
don't mean shit
without a golden bedpost
to tie yourself to

breadcrumbs
and a knife in the bed
still smeared with butter
yellow grease
against the sheets

her confidence
darkened like a sunset
orange and violet
she lunged
at some memory of herself
hair tangled with
blue salt beside the sea

lovers
of themselves and their hungers
the foreign tourists laughed
told the taxi driver to go
as slow as possible
and asked him to put out
his cigarette.

"Because no one of substance ever dared testify. In Krupskaya's words, the revelations would be catastrophic for governments everywhere. Now, there are new tactics being employed, all for the purpose of creating instability in the power centers."

"What are they?"

"Acts of terrorism. Bombings, kidnappings, the hijacking of aircraft; ultimatums issued by bands of fanatics, wholesale slaughter promised if they are not met. They grow in numbers every month and the vast majority are funded by the Matarese."

"How?"

"I can only surmise. The Matarese council studies the objectives of the parties involved, sends in the experts, and provides covert financing. Fanatics do not labor over the sources of funds, only their availability. I submit that you and I have used such men and women more often than we can count."

"For distinctly accountable purposes," said Bray, picking up his cup from the floor. "What about Blackburn and Yurievich? What did the Matarese accomplish by killing them?"

"Krupskaya believed it was to test the leaders, to see if their own men could control each government's reactions. I'm not so sure now. I think perhaps there was something else. Frankly, because of what you've told me."

"What's that?"

"Yurievich. You said he was your operation. Is that true?"

Bray frowned. "True, but not that simple. Yurievich was gray; he wasn't going to defect in any normal sense. He was a scientist, convinced both sides had gone too far. He didn't trust the maniacs. It was a probe; we weren't sure where we were going."

"Are you aware that General Blackburn, who was nearly destroyed by the war in Vietnam did what no Chairman of the Joint Chiefs has ever done in your history? He met secretly with your potential enemies. In Sweden, in the city of Skelleftea on the Gulf of Bothnia, traveling undercover as a tourist. It was our judgment that he would go to any lengths to avoid the repetition of pointless slaughter. He abhorred conventional warfare, and he did not believe nuclear weapons would ever be used." The Russian stopped and leaned forward. "Two men who believed deeply,

181

181
Testify:
being, purpose, power
can be
acts of terrorism
bombing kidnapping hijacks
funded by
narratives of self-actualization
the old austere mythologies
succumb to the lust of cash transactions

I have used such men
to subdue the stockyards
of civilization
they break easily
upon a bleating neck

test reactions
for signs of authenticity
the Pavlovian genital jingle
gets the cat's attention
every time

true
instinct is a horse drinking water
but normal perceptions fall
with the first hammer blow

probe
the historical record you will find
the war in Vietnam
was a dry run for mass
historical revisionism
slaughter was conventional
to the point of
banality
and the men who believed
lit their cigars and
watched it like a fox hunt.

THE MATARESE CIRCLE

down the side of the manmade rivulet to the first path, an alleyway, bordered on both sides by what appeared to be hundreds of stone statues spewing arcs of water in unison. The floodlights filtered through the trees; the scene was eerily peaceful, juxtaposed to but not affected by the stampeding chaos from the terraces above.

"Straight through!" said Scofield. "At the end there's a waterfall and another staircase. It'll get us back up there."

They started running through the tunnel of foliage, mist from the arcs of water joining the sweat on their faces.

"*Dannazione!*" Antonia fell, the long black cape torn from her shoulders by a branch of sapling. Bray stopped and pulled her up.

"*Ecco la!*"

"*La donna!*"

Shouts came from behind them; gunshots followed. Two men came running through the water-filled alleyway; they were targets, silhouetted by the light from the fountain beyond. Scofield fired three rounds. One man fell, holding his thigh; the second grabbed his shoulder, his gun flying out of his hand as he dove for the protection of the nearest statue.

Bray and Antonia reached the staircase at the end of the path. An entrance of the villa. They ran up, taking the steps two at a time, until they joined the panicked crowds rushing out through the enclosed courtyard into the huge parking lot.

Chauffeurs were everywhere, standing by elegant automobiles, protecting them, waiting for sight of their employers—and as with all chauffeurs in Italy in these times, their guns were drawn; protection was everything. They had been schooled; they were prepared.

One, however, was not prepared enough. Bray approached him.

"Is this Count Scozzi's car?" he asked breathlessly.

"No, it is not, signore! Stand back!"

"Sorry." Scofield took a step away from the man, sufficiently to allay his fears, then lunged forward, hammering the barrel of his automatic into the side of the chauffeur's skull. The man collapsed.

"Get in!" he yelled to Antonia. "Lock the doors and stay on the floor until we're out of here."

335

335
the manmade rivulet
splashed between his feet
stone statues
erode beneath the piss
of centuries
juxtaposed
with the shadows of bird migrations
passing overhead

running through the tunnel
we were
silhouetted by light
from the mouth of the cave
the newest idol
is the one
with the freshest
splash of blood

chauffeurs
huddle together
like a school
of blinded fish
perfectly correct
wiping flecks of
spittle from their lips
submission
automatic
as a dog fetching a stick
and panting to be praised

we're out of honey bees
and we've felled the groves
that gave us sugar
that gave shade to the
stone statues by the stream

minerals fade from memory
but recombine
as blossoms
rooted in the shallow loam
of leaves and bones.

THE MATARESE CIRCLE

MATARSE CIRCULO ~~(to a kinder, gentler regime)~~

"Tell that clown to shut up, Bray!" shouted the technician at the table.

"You heard the man," said Scofield, focusing on the spires of the buildings outside. "You just lost the upgrade. Your outrageous statement that we intend to commit bodily harm tarnishes our friends in the Company."

The younger man grimaced. The rebuke was deserved. "Sorry. It still doesn't make sense. That cipher was a priority alert; we should take him tonight."

Scofield lowered the binoculars and looked at Harry. "I'll tell you what *does* make sense," he said. "Somewhat more than those silly godamned phrases someone found on the back of a cereal box. That man down there was terrified. He hasn't slept in days. He's strung out to the breaking point, and I want to know why."

"There could be a dozen reasons," countered the younger man. "He's old. Inexperienced. Maybe he thinks we're on to him, that he's about to be caught. What difference does it make?"

"A man's life, that's all."

"Come on, Bray, not from *you*. He's Soviet poison; a double-agent."

"I want to be sure."

"And I want to get out of here," broke in the technician, handing Scofield a reel of tape and picking up his machine. "Tell the clown we never met."

"Thanks, Mr. No-name. I owe you." The CIA man left, nodding at Bray, avoiding any contact with his associate.

"There was no one here but us chickens, Harry," said Scofield after the door was shut. "You do understand that."

"He's a nasty bastard—"

"Who could tap the White House toilets, if he hasn't already," said Bray, tossing the reel of tape to Harry. "Get our unsolicited indictments over to the embassy. Take out the film and leave the camera here."

Harry would not be put off; he caught the reel of tape, but made no move toward the camera. "I'm in this, too. That cipher applied

39

39
The technician
punched in the codes but
due to hardware limitations
lost the upgrade
to a kinder gentler regime

the need
to commit bodily harm
had been obsolete for decades
but the old-school sadists
remained
take him tonight
an officer said
and somewhere
a barrel of tar was already bubbling
above a fire at the end of a road

the silly goddamned phrases
we had to swallow like our own vomit
seemed to kill me from inside-out
the breaking point
was insane boredom
a bored insanity
that made men want to
tear out their eyes

a man's life
ended up being no more than a
totem pole in a forest fire

the Soviet poison
came in the same vial as the US toxin
just with a different label
no identifying features
it was the only thing the
Americans didn't stick their flag on

The CIA
was so post-coitally arrogant

in those days
they made a prototype of
White House toilets
that rammed shit
into visitors' assholes rather than
flushing it away

the embassy
never answered the phone
just traced the calls
and sent data to the technicians
the camera
became an invisible ubiquitous eye
that convinced whole populations
they were having fun.

THE MATARESE CIRCLE

The Greek studied Vasili in the dim light. "So the great Taleniekov flees Russia. He can remain only as a corpse."

"Not from Russia, only from frightened men. But I do have to leave—for a while. I've got to figure out how."

"There is a way," said the merchant seaman simply. "We'll head over the northwest coast, then south into the mountains. You'll be in Greece in three days."

"How?"

"There's a convoy of trucks that go first to Odessa. . . ."

Taleniekov sat on the hard bench in the back of the truck, the light of dawn seeping through the billowing canvas flaps that covered the sides. In a while, he and the others would have to crawl beneath the floor boards, remaining motionless and silent on a concealed ledge between the axles, while they passed through the next checkpoint. But for an hour or so they could stretch and breathe air that did not reek of oil and grease.

He reached into his pocket and took out the cipher from Washington, the cable that had already cost three lives.

Invitation Kasimir. Schrankenwarten five goals, Unter den Linden. Przseslvac zero. Prague. Repeat text. Zero. Repeat again at will. Zero.

Beowulf Agate.

Two codes. One meaning.

With his pen, Vasili wrote out that meaning beneath the cipher.

Come and take me, as you took someone else across a checkpoint at five o'clock on the Unter den Linden. I've broken and killed your courier, as another courier was killed in Prague. Repeat: Come to me. I'll kill you.

Scofield

Beyond the American killer's brutal decision, the most electrifying aspect of Scofield's cable was the fact that he was no longer in

107

107
Remain as a corpse to hide
from frightened men
sometimes it's the only way
to keep from falling
to despond

the merchant seaman
offered me a swig of rum and said
in three days go to Odesa
check in to the Tivoli Hotel
and wait for your contact
a hooker who refuses
to be paid
fuck her if you want
nobody cares
what happens behind that door—
he peeled off his fake beard
revealing a face like a
dead fish

if you crawl beneath the floor boards
and stay silent
you may feel safe but
the axles of war
keep turning
with their stench of oil and grease
civilian populations
lubricate the gears

Prague
in a whole afternoon I made
zero centimes busking on the Charles Bridge
my guitar was drowned by national anthems
and military bands
one meaning
of loaded dice is a desire to win
but another is hopelessness
in the face of destiny
not to mention a lack of courtesy

I've broken
everything inside myself
that I wanted to give to you
it wasn't hard
your absence
did most of the job

the American killer
felt naked and confused
no longer able
to control his face or eyes
he took another shot of rum and
smoothed the false beard back
around his lips.

THE MATARESE CIRCLE

you to understand. We found you; we'll always be able to find you. But it's all so tedious. We feel that it would be far better for everyone concerned if we sat down and thrashed out the differences between us. You may discover they're not so great after all."

"I don't feel comfortable with people who've tried to kill me."

"I must correct you. *Some* have tried to kill you. Others have tried to save you."

"For what? A session of chemical therapy? To find out what I've learned, what I've done?"

"What you've learned is meaningless, and you can't *do* anything. If your own people take you, you know what you can expect. There'll be no trial, no public hearing; you're far too dangerous to too many people. You've collaborated with the enemy, killed a young man your superiors believe was a fellow intelligence officer in Rock Creek Park, and fled the country. You're a traitor; you'll be executed at the first opportune moment. Can you doubt it after the events on Nebraska Avenue? *We* can execute you the instant you walk out of that restaurant. Or before you leave."

Bray looked around, studying the faces at the tables, looking for the inevitable pair of eyes, a glance behind a folded newspaper, or above the rim of a coffee cup. There were several candidates; he could not be sure. And without question, there were unseen killers in the crowds outside. He was trapped; his watch read eleven minutes past ten. Another four and he could dial Symonds on the sterile line. But he was dealing with professionals. If he hung up and dialed was there a man now at one of these tables—innocuously raising a fork to his mouth or sipping from a cup—who would pull out a weapon powerful enough to blow him into the wall? Or were those inside merely hired guns, unwilling to make the sacrifice the Matarese demanded of its élite? He had to buy time and take the risk, watching the tables every second as he did so, preparing himself for that instant when escape came with sudden movement and the conceivable—unfortunate—sacrifice of innocent people.

"You want to meet, I want a guarantee I'll get out of here."

451
we'll always find you
tedious
sorry to say
in your gray houndstooth coat
and charcoal tie
everyone has a chance to
discover they're not expendable
every mote of every dream is essential to the whole
despite uncontrolled nuclear escalation
surging through the fevered lymph nodes
of the dictators
chemical therapy
doesn't change the fact that
what you've learned is meaningless
who would remonstrate if you broke a taboo
if you killed a fellow intelligence

kicking through the sunset autumn leaves of
Nebraska Avenue
or sprawling on a Pacific atoll
sifting bleached coral fragments
through your fingers
we are a world of
unseen killers
blithely raising forks up to our mouths
hunger a greater weapon
than games of chicken with mushroom clouds
make the sacrifice
pull the skin from your hand like a glove
escape
the conventional weapons
of artifice and civility

I want a guarantee
that my head is
exploding for a good cause
hey it's
451
all over again
this time
with no books left to burn.

THE MATARESE CIRCLE

twenty feet from the edge. Several hundred yards below, he had seen the glow of a cigarette. The road was being guarded; he had waited. He had to.

If Scofield was coming he would use that road; it had been the dawn of the fourth day. The American had said that if Corsica was all that was left, he'd be there in three or four days.

By three in the afternoon there had been no sign of him, and an hour later Vasili knew he could wait no longer. Men had sped down the road toward the burgeoning port resort. Their mission had been clear: the intruder had eluded the road block. Find him, kill him.

Search parties had begun fanning through the woods; two Corsicans slashing the overgrowth with mountain machetes had come within thirty feet of him; soon the patrols would become more concentrated, the search more thorough. He could not wait for Scofield; there was no guarantee that Beowulf Agate had even escaped from the net being spread for him in his own country, much less on his way to Corsica.

Vasili had spent the hours until sundown creating his own assaults on those who would trap him. Like a swamp fox, his trail appeared one moment heading in *this* direction, his appearance sighted over *there;* broken limbs and trampled reeds were proof that he was cornered in a stretch of marshland that fronted an unclimbable wall of schist, and as men closed in, his figure could be seen racing through a field a mile to the west. He was a yellow jacket on the wind, visually stinging in a dozen different places at once.

When darkness had come, Taleniekov had begun the strategy that led him to where he was at the moment, hidden in a cluster of fir trees below the crown of a high hill, waiting for a man carrying a flashlight to approach. The plan was simple, carried out in three stages, each phase logically evolved from the previous one. First came the diversion, drawing off the largest number of the attack pack as possible; then the exposure to the few left behind, pulling them farther away from the many; finally the separation of those few and the trapping of one. The third phase was about to be concluded as the fires raged a mile and a half below to the east.

211
from the edge
of the cliff men watched as
the road waited below
like a shed snakeskin
wrinkled by bomb craters

the American said
he could wait no longer
to call in the shock troops
the intruder had already
been dead two days
he'd come
slashing
through the media circus
with images of banal atrocity
like pissing on a child's ice cream cone

it had seemed not quite sporting
to play by different rules than those
of the oligarchs

now he was a mash of
broken limbs
and his blood turned black
in the desert sun
we had been
racing
against radio signals and surveillance drones
to find a
visually soothing avatar of the war
something everyone who agreed with us
could agree upon

the plan was simple
emotionless
logically evolved
a moral stoichiometry
of clean hands

finally the separation
between us and other
could not be denied
as the fires raged
through the dark
that would never feel again.

THE MATARESE CIRCLE

"It didn't just *happen*. *How* did it happen?"

"I can only tell you what I heard. A man came to the leaders—several were in jail. He told them to find him when they got out on the streets again. He could lead them to large sources of money that could be made without the heavy risks involved in robbery and kidnapping."

"In other words," said Scofield, thinking rapidly as he spoke, "he offered to finance them in a major way with minor effort. Teams of two people going out for three or four weeks—and returning with something like nine million lire. Seventy thousand dollars for a month's work. Minimum risk, maximum return. Very few personnel involved."

"Yes. In the beginning, the contacts came from him, that man. They in turn led to others. As you say, it does not take many people and they bring in large amounts of money."

"So the Brigades can concentrate on their true calling," completed Bray sardonically. "The disruption of the social order. In a single word, terrorism." He got up from the bed. "That man who came to see the leaders in jail. Did he stay in touch with them?"

She frowned. "Again, I can only tell you what I heard. He was never seen after the second meeting."

"I'll bet he wasn't. Every negotiation always five times removed from the source. . . . A geometric progression, no single line to retrace. That's how they do it."

"Who?"

"The Matarese."

Antonia stared at him. "Why do you say that?"

"Because it's the only explanation. Serious dealers in narcotics wouldn't *touch* maniacs like the Brigades. It's a controlled situation, a charade mounted to finance terrorism, so the Matarese can continue to finance the guns and the killing. In Italy it's the Red Brigades; in Germany, Baader-Meinhof; in Lebanon, the PLO; in my country, the Minutemen and the Weathermen, the Ku Klux Klan and the JDL and all the godamn fools who blew up banks and laboratories and embassies. Each financed differently, secretly. All pawns for the Matarese—maniacal pawns, and that's the scary thing. The longer they're fed the bigger they grow, and the bigger

299

299
It didn't happen
like they told it
but the witnesses were dressed
differently
from the crowd
no one believed anything
without the heavy
jowls of the status quo
hanging down like slabs
of meat

nine million
lives in a city
or grains of sugar in a cup
are easily dissolved and allowed
to drain away

was the disruption of the social order
terrorism
or liberation
ask the animals
or the children
in their cages
a geometric progression
offers no hope
only spiking debt
trading bone for bone
on the slaughterhouse floor

you can't plot escape from
the guns and the killing
with a compass and
slide rule any more
laboratories and embassies
have all the exits covered
the bigger fish escape but it's no
salvation
for those inside their
bellies.

THE MATARESE CIRCLE

the product of two terminated intelligence officers—both wanted for treason in their respective countries. The time *would* come, but it was not now. For the truth of the matter was that they did not possess a shred of hard evidence. Everything they knew to be true was so easily denied as the paranoid ramblings of lunatics and traitors. On the surface, the logic was their enemies'. Why would the leaders of mammoth corporations, conglomerates that depended on stability, finance chaos?

Chaos. Formless matter, clashing bodies in space....

"Another few minutes, we'll reach our first destination," said Israel Isles.

"First destination?"

"Yes, our trip's in two stages. We change vehicles up ahead; this one is driven back to London—the driver black, his passenger white—and we proceed in another, quite different car. The next leg is less than a quarter of an hour. Mr. Symonds may be a little late, however. He had to make four changes of vehicles in city garages."

"I see," said Scofield, relieved. The West Indian had just provided Bray with his answer. As the rendezvous with Symonds was in stages, so, too, would be the explanation *to* Symonds. He would tell him part of the truth, but nothing that would implicate the Foreign Secretary, David Waverly. However, Waverly had to be given information on a most confidential basis; decisions of foreign policy could be affected by the news of massive shifts of capital being manipulated secretly. *This* was the information Scofield had come across and was tracing: massive shifts of capital. And although all clandestine economic maneuvers were subjects for intelligence scrutiny, these went beyond MI-5 and 6, just as they superseded the interests of the FBI and the CIA.

In Washington, there were those who wanted to prevent him from disclosing what he knew, but could not prove. The surest way of doing so was to discredit him, kill him, if it came to that. Symonds would understand. Men killed facilely for money; no one knew it better than intelligence officers. So often it was the spine of their . . . accomplishments.

441

441
terminated intelligence
is a means of quelling
treason
whoring truth
out for the jingle of political coin
ramblings of lunatics
become infallible logic
mammoth corporations joust over
formless matter
archaic ways of being sink
into the hush of ocean waves

change vehicles
when a better tax credit
or messiah appears
less than a quarter
of humanity
owns a pair of shoes
or flosses regularly
but the presidents unveil
new multi-billion dollar suits
of body armor
to protect against dandruff and bad
breath

massive protests in the
capital
won concessions from the president
to install robot toilets in every home
but clandestine economic surveillance
would be gathered with every
flush

if you meet the buddha
kill
the buddha

the time of increase does not endure
break the
spine
of the book you wrote
watch the pages
scatter.

---

the time of increase...from the *I-Ching*.

THE MATARESE CIRCLE

prominent man, a resourceful man. Give me a letter of certification and get me into the Records of Property."

The German shook his head. "No, I won't do that. You wouldn't know what to look for. But you may accompany me."

"You'd do this yourself? Why?"

"I despise extremists who deal in violence. I remember too vividly the screams and diatribes of the Third Reich. I shall, indeed, look for myself, and if we get lucky you can tell me what you wish." Kassel lightened his voice, but sadness was there. "Besides, anyone sentenced to death by Moscow cannot be all bad. Now, tell me the name."

Taleniekov stared at the attorney, seeing another sentence of death. "Voroshin," he said.

The uniformed clerk in the Essen Hall of Records treated the prominent Heinrich Kassel with extreme deference. Herr Kassel's firm was one of the most important in the city. He made it plain that the coarse-looking receptionist behind the desk would be delighted to make copies of anything Herr Kassel wished to have duplicated. The woman stared up unpleasantly, her expression disapproving.

The steel file cabinets in the enormous room that housed the Records of Property were like gray robots stacked one on top of the other, circling the room, staring down at the open cubicles where the certified lawyers did their research.

"Everything is recorded by date," said Kassel. "Year, month, day. Be as specific as you can. What was the earliest Voroshin might have reasonably bought property in the Essen districts?"

"Allowing for the slow methods of travel at the time, say late May or early June of 1911. But I told you, he wouldn't have bought under his own name."

"We won't be looking for his name, or even an assumed name. Not to begin with."

"Why not an assumed name? Why couldn't he buy what was available under another name if he had the funds?"

"Because of the times, and they haven't changed that much. A man does not simply enter a community with his family and

403

403
prominent
men sit atop the pyramid
counting coins
from high interest loans
they keep
extremists who deal in violence
on a long leash
secure in the knowledge that
the Third Reich
was no anomaly
in the arc of human history
but sadness leaks in all the same
through the corks of the champagne magnums
mixing with the bubbles like
another sentence of death
as the tennis shots go
pock. pock. pock.
on the other side of the hedges
strung with razor wire

extreme deference
to the terms of lascivious dictatorship
has always been the path to easy fortune
a deck chair in the sun

the woman stared up unpleasantly
the men laughed like
gray robots
certified lawyers
with qualifications tattooed on
their members
which they brandished at the slightest provocation

the arson attack on
slow methods
of breathing
raised the futures price for gold teeth
we won't be looking for
perpetrators the magistrate said

the assumed machineries will collect
the funds
to disburse at their discretion

as the superyachts
float empty
beyond the horizon
far out at sea.

THE MATARESE CIRCLE

The ringing on the telephone was now abrasive. Long sudden bursts resulting from a furious operator punching a switchboard button. There was no answer and Vasili began to think the unthinkable: Beowulf Agate had intercepted his bait. If so, the American was in greater danger than he could imagine. Three men had flown in from Europe to be his executioners, and—no less lethal—a gentle-appearing old woman whom he might try to compromise would kill him the instant she felt cornered. He would never know where the shot came from, nor that she even had a weapon.

"I'm sorry, sir!" said the operator angrily. "There's still no pick-up in suite two-eleven. I suggest you call again." She did not wait for a reply; the switchboard line was disconnected.

The *switchboard*? The *operator*?

It was a desperate tactic, one he would never condone except as a last-extremity measure; the risk of exposure was too great. But it *was* the last extremity, and if there were alternatives he was too exhausted to think of them. Again, he knew only that he had to act, each decision an instinctive reflex, the shaping of those instincts trusted. He reached into his pocket for his money and removed five one-hundred dollar bills. Then he took out his passport case, and extracted a letter he had written on an English-language typewriter five days ago in Moscow. The letterhead was that of a brokerage house in Bern; it identified the bearer as one of the firm's partners. One never knew. . . .

He walked out of the telephone booth and entered the flow of pedestrians until he was directly opposite the entrance of the hotel. He waited for a break in the traffic, then walked rapidly across Nebraska Avenue.

Two minutes later a solicitous day manager introduced a Monsieur Blanchard to the operator of the hotel switchboard. This same manager—as impressed with Monsieur Blanchard's credentials as he was with the two hundred dollars the Swiss financier had casually insisted he take for his troubles—dutifully provided a relief operator while the woman talked alone with the generous Monsieur Blanchard.

139

139
the telephone was abrasive
a tentacled operator
with shattered glass
in place of suction cups
knurling through my brain
like an eddy of liquid sandpaper
the executioners
had to be amused
at how little was left for them to do

love was a weapon
in the hands of the operator
blandly plugging in
connections
of landscapes melted into silicon
touching lips to lips

teeth and tongues devolve into
the last extremity
of hope
before the line goes dead

the sexual instincts trusted
one-hundred dollar bills
and mortar rounds above
the gulf stream and ocean currents

it was raining in Moscow
when the doors
of a brokerage house were smashed open
to a stench of gasoline
the telephone
wired to a detonation cap
as children on the street
sang Christmas carols
and held a hat collecting coins

I called the operator
just to hear a human voice

but the sound was mechanical as a Swiss financier
smoking Gauloises and steering a Mercedes-Benz
the operator
loved me more than anyone in the world
with a logic I could not
resist.

THE MATARESE CIRCLE

The voices were muffled, but intense. He could hear the words *police* and *ambulance*, and then *emergency*. There were three or four people.

Bray yanked the door back and pushed the bell captain out into the corridor. "*Now*," he said.

Taleniekov turned away as the service elevator opened on the second floor. Again the black overcoat and the distinctive gray hat evoked no sounds of recognition, and again he spun, his hand gripping the Graz-Burya in his pocket. There were tray tables of half-eaten food and the odor of coffee—remnants of late breakfasts piling up outside the elevator door—but no Marseilles.

A pair of hinged metal doors opened into the second-floor corridor, round windows in the center of each panel. Vasili approached and peered through the right circle.

There he was. The figure in the heavy tweed suit was edging his way along the wall toward the corner of the intersecting hallway that led to room 213. Taleniekov looked at his watch; it was 12:31. Four minutes until the attack; a lifetime if Scofield kept his head about him. A diversion was needed; fire was the surest. A telephone call, a flaming pillowcase stuffed with cloth and paper thrown into the hallway. He wondered if Beowulf Agate had thought of it.

Scofield had thought of *something*. Down the hall the light above one of the two main elevators went on; the door opened, and three men rushed out talking frantically. One was the manager, now close to panic; another carried a black bag: a doctor. The third, was burly, his face set, the hair close-cropped . . . the hotel's private police officer.

They raced past the startled Marseilles—who turned abruptly away—and proceeded down the long corridor that led to Scofield's room. The Frenchman took out a gun.

At the other end of the hallway, below a red *Exit* sign, a heavy door with a crash bar was pulled back. The figure of Prague stepped out, nodding at Marseilles. In his right hand was a long-barreled, heavy-caliber automatic, in his left what looked like . . .

163

163

it's a muffled emergency
a pair of gasoline-soaked boxer shorts
stuffed in your mouth as a gag
a tray of scones and teacups
is the fuse

the condemned man in the black overcoat
lit a cigarette
and slipped pastries in his pocket
his throat half-eaten
by esophageal cancer
as he locked the hinged metal
brace around his groin

I always moved in the right circles
and in the steeplechase concourse
the champagne flutes were bottomless
until the attack
when the horses screamed
and we wished for nothing but a
flaming pillow
on which to lay our heads
as we slept and dreamed
of a futureless past

I carried my thoughts in a black bag
and locked them in a
Penn Station luggage compartment
then sent the key to a fortune teller
in Tangiers

walk the long corridor
naked and shivering
love and desperation
can't be told apart by the metal floor
or by the guard with his
heavy-caliber genitals
who paces outside the door
and pounds it with his rifle butt
when you scream.

MATARSE CIRCULO

had buried his attaché case and duffle bag. They traveled cautiously, using the woods as much as possible, separating and walking in sequence across open stretches so no one would see them together.

Scofield pulled the shovel from beneath a pile of branches, dug up his belongings, and they started out again, retracing the stream north toward Sainte Lucie. Conversation was kept to a minimum; they wasted no time putting distance between themselves and the hills.

The long silences and brief separations served a practical purpose, thought Bray, watching the girl as she pressed forward, bewildered, following their commands without thinking, tears intermittently appearing in her eyes. The constant movement occupied her mind; she had to come to some sort of acceptance of her "grandmother"'s death. No words from relative strangers could help her; she needed the loneliness of her own thoughts. Scofield suspected that in spite of her handling of the Lupo, Antonia was not a child of violence. She was no child to begin with; in the daylight he could see that she would not see thirty again, but beyond that, she came from a world of radical academics, not revolution. He doubted she would know what to do at the barricades.

"We must stop *running!*" she cried suddenly. "You may do what you like, but I am returning to Porto Vecchio. I'll see them *hanged!*"

"There's a great deal you don't know," said Taleniekov.

"She was killed! That is all I *have* to know!"

"It's not that simple," said Bray. "The truth is she killed herself."

"*They* killed her!"

"She forced them to." Scofield took her hand, gripping it firmly. "Try to understand me. We can't let you go back; your grandmother knew that. What happened during the past forty-eight hours has got to fade away just as fast as possible. There'll be a certain amount of panic up in those hills; they'll send men trying to find us, but in several weeks when nothing happens, they'll cool

261
I was tired of running
I missed my dog and my wife's cooking
though he was dead and she was gone
I buried my passport
beneath a pile of leaves
a futile gesture amid
long silences and brief separations
grown permanent as stone
but all gestures are futile when
appearing in her eyes
nothing else remains

the loneliness of her own thoughts
became a formula

even blinded by shrapnel
in the daylight he could see his
world of revolution
had been marauder's blood lust
since it tried to kill the leaves on trees
and the silence of snowed-in mountains
she tried to kill me
I kissed her anyway
with bloody teeth
I don't remember what happened
only why

my handler always said
nothing happens by accident
but even he wouldn't bother
throwing himself chest-down
on a grenade
unless he knew it was live
and would take his whole world in a flash.

miles south of Bastia. Her immediate contribution was to get them there without being seen. It was important that she make decisions, if only to take her mind off the fact that she was following orders she disagreed with. She did so rapidly, choosing primitive back roads and mountain trails she had known as a child growing up in the province.

"The nuns brought us here for a picnic," she said, looking down at a dammed-up stream. "We built fires and ate sausage, and took turns going into the woods to smoke cigarettes."

They went on. "This hill has a fine wind in the morning," she said. "My father made marvelous kites and we would fly them here on Sundays. After Mass, of course."

"We?" asked Bray. "Do you have brothers and sisters?"

"One of each. They're older than I am and still live in Vescovato. They have families and I do not see them often; there's not much to talk about between us."

"They didn't go to the upper schools then?" said Taleniekov.

"They thought such pursuits were foolish. They're good people but prefer a simple life. If we need help, they will offer it."

"It would be better not to seek it," said the Russian. "Or them."

"They are my family, signore. Why should I avoid them?"

"Because it may be necessary."

"That's no answer. You kept me from Porto Vecchio and the justice that should be done; you can't give me orders any longer."

The KGB man looked at Scofield, his intent in his eyes. Bray expected the Russian to draw his weapon. He wondered briefly what his own reaction would be; he could not tell. But the moment passed, and Scofield understood something he had not fully understood before. Vasili Taleniekov did not wish to kill, but the professional in him was in strong conflict with the man. The Russian was pleading with him. He wanted to know how to convert a liability into an asset. Scofield wished he knew.

"Take it easy," said Bray. "Nobody wants to tell you what to do except where your own safety's concerned. We said that before and it's ten times more valid now."

263

263
My feet were mangled by the tank tracks
otherwise I came through unscathed
but I lost equilibrium forever
even lying in the uncut grass
as farm girls lead cows home through the trees
as clouds turn to roses in the sky
I can feel the earth has listed into sadness
from which it will never rise again
not because it can't
but because it no longer wishes to.

THE MATARESE CIRCLE
MATARSE CIRCULO

eyes automatically riveted on an indented clause on the first page, "here's another. A cousin of the Krupps is transferring ownership of property in Rellinghausen to a woman in Düsseldorf in gratitude for her many years of service. Really!"

"It's possible, isn't it?"

"Of course not; the family would never permit it. A relative found a way to turn a handsome profit by selling to someone who did not want his peers—or his creditors—to know he had the money. Someone who controlled the woman in Düsseldorf, if she ever existed. The Krupps probably congratulated their cousin."

And so it went. 1911, 1912, 1913, 1914 . . . 1915.

August 20, 1915.

The name was there. It meant nothing to Heinrich Kassel, but it did to Taleniekov. It brought to mind another document 2,000 miles away in the archives in Leningrad. The crimes of the Voroshin family, the intimate associates of Prince Andrei.

Friedrich Schotte.

"Wait a minute!" Vasili placed his hand over the pages. "Where's this?"

"Stadtwald. There's nothing irregular here. As a matter of fact, it's absolutely legal, very clean."

"Perhaps too legal, too clean. Just as the Voroshin massacre was too profuse with detail."

"What in God's name are you talking about?"

"What do you know of this Friedrich Schotte?"

The attorney grimaced in thought, trying to recall irrelevant history; this was not what he was looking for. "He worked for the Krupps, I think, in a very high position. It would have had to be for him to buy this. He got in trouble after the First World War. I don't remember the circumstances—a prison sentence, or something—but I can't see why it's relevant."

"I can," said Taleniekov. "He was convicted of manipulating money out of Germany. He was killed on the first night of that prison sentence in 1919. Was the estate sold then?"

"I would think so. It would appear by the map survey to be a rather expensive property for a prison widow to maintain."

"How can we find out?"

405

405
eyes automatically riveted
on automated images
flipped and clicked in
years of service to
automaton patterns
of thought
in fealty to hegemons
and guillotines

the Krupps
went from artillery and bullets to
espresso machines
the profit was the same
the archives in Leningrad
were conveniently destroyed
the scion
placed his hand
on her groin
as his grandfather had done
absolutely legal, very clean
in the terms of the corporate hierarchy

why not use
God's name
to make a few bucks it doesn't
cost Him anything
irrelevant history
to the jubilation of
perpetual World War
it's all in His name His glory
exfoliations
in the pages of the empire's
automated history
the map survey was never
intended as anything but
a prison
for alternative ways of being
how can we
breathe

while the animals weep in cages
the system maps your thoughts automatically
a digital rivet for every synapse
a leaf of virtual love for every bone.

THE MATARESE CIRCLE
MATARSE CIRCULO

The woman opened her file folder and scanned the top page before speaking. She turned to the second page and addressed the Premier, her eyes avoiding the diplomat. "As you know, there were two assassins, presumably both male. One had to be a marksman of extreme skill and coordination, the other someone who undoubtedly possessed the same qualifications, but who was also an expert in electronic surveillance. There was evidence in the stables—bracket scrapings, suction imprints, footprints indicating unobstructed vantage points—that lead us to believe all conversations in the *dacha* were intercepted."

"You describe CIA expertise, comrade," interrupted the Premier.

"Or Consular Operations, sir," replied the woman. "It's important to bear that in mind."

"Oh, yes," agreed the Premier. "The State Department's small band of negotiators."

"Why not the Chinese Tao-pans?" offered the diplomat earnestly. "They're among the most effective killers on earth. The Chinese had more to fear from Yurievich than anyone else."

"Physiognomy rules them out," countered the man from VKR. "If one was caught, even after cyanide, Peking knows it would be destroyed."

"Get back to this pattern you've found," interrupted the Premier.

The woman continued. "We fed everything through KGB computers, concentrating on American intelligence personnel we know have penetrated Russia, who speak the language fluently, and are known killers. We have arrived at four names. Here they are, Mr. Premier. Three from the Central Intelligence Agency, one from the Department of State's Consular Operations." She handed the page to the VKR man, who in turn rose and gave it to the Premier.

He looked at the names.

Scofield, Brandon Alan. State Department, Consular Operations. Known to have been responsible for assassinations in Prague, Athens, Paris, Munich. Suspected of having operated

31
I feel like a strange animal
trapped between the lines of someone else's book
trapped between institution walls
constructed to define me
what do I kill
what am I dying for
contract subtract redact refract compact
what is strange and what is normal
the world can't help you any more
if life is a bowling alley is it normal to be
the ball or the pins
each is complicit to inevitable decay
spin to me with your mass of destruction
fall to my touch to stand into regimentation again
I am still dying
and she is still alive and free beyond
some black horizon
and my books are strange animals
roaming a wilderness
beyond anyone's hands or teeth
as the monkeys scream
and claw the mesh screens of their cages
the screens of their cages
on the metro
with faces like wet black petals on a bough
the cages of our screens
spinning and falling
through the pages of someone else's book
tired but can't sleep
hungry but can't eat
tap the screen to pull up your bank account
transfer some funds
book a holiday cruise
book a family vacation
buy a new stethoscope
buy a new car
buy a military service deferment
buy a shattered mirror
hold the shards in place with spit and jism

and silicon lubricant
lace up your bowling shoes and walk down Main Street
let the pins
fall where they may.

*

there was one secret left
till robots dug the earth up to reveal it

gunships came looming down
their shadows passed across the naked skin
of bathers on the beach
then turned back when
none remained to oppose them

she walked through
the wasteland of disbelief
past fossil sculptures of decay
and tossed breadcrumbs
to a shark in a goldfish pond

low class but in a good way
the trees and busboys know my name

my teeth and tongue are stained with wine
the doctor tells me to buy another machine

Scott Ezell is a Pacific Rim poet and multi-genre artist with a background in Asia and Indigenous peoples. He has published more than ten books of poetry and nonfiction and over a dozen collections of original folk, ambient, and experimental music, including most recently the album *The Television Will Not Be Revolutionized*.

This project was conceived and produced in San Cristóbal de las Casas, Chiapas, Mexico, in 2022, with an old Olivetti typewriter and cut-out pages of a Cold War spy novel. It was published in an initial hand-made edition of twelve copies.

scottezell.com